Old Newcastle
by Hugh Oram

Main Street, looking south, 1935. On the left-hand side are a line of shops starting with an embroidery and Irish linen shop (now Hale's fruit shop). On the same side can be seen St Mary's Roman Catholic Church, built in the late 1840s on a site donated by the Annesley estate. Before it was built, Mass had been said in a temporary chapel in King Street, on the southern side of the town. St Mary's remained in use until the present Our Lady of Assumption Church, with its wigwam shaped roof, was dedicated in 1966 by the late Most Rev. Dr William Philbin, Bishop of Down and Connor. St Mary's is now used as a youth centre and as an indoor skateboard facility, the latter opening in 2006.

Text © Hugh Oram, 2007.
First published in the United Kingdom, 2008,
by Stenlake Publishing Ltd.
Telephone: 01290 551122
www.stenlake.co.uk
ISBN 9781840334203

The publishers regret that they cannot supply
copies of any pictures featured in this book.

Acknowledgements

The publishers wish to thank Des Quail for contributing photographs to this book.

The author wishes to thank the following: Terence Bowman, Editor, the *Mourne Observer*; Tom Walsh, Newcastle; Denis Murphy and John Kennedy, Newcastle Art Gallery; James Laidler, Secretary, Royal County Down Golf Club; Lesley Simpson, Keeper of Collections, Down County Museum; Peter Law and Eileen Bannon, Newcastle Chamber of Commerce; Karina Meredith and Stuart Walsh, Northern Ireland Water; Sandes Soldiers' and Airmens' Homes, Belfast; Berrie O'Neill, the Percy French Society; James Davidson, Lambeg; Niamh Stephenson, RNLI Ireland; Hugh Paul, RNLI, Newcastle; Neil Mahony, Scouting Ireland; Ken Gillespie, Scouting Association of Northern Ireland; Deon McNeilly, 1st Newcastle Scouts; Sharon Pollock, Glenada YMCA, Newcastle; Bill Martin, Newcastle; Stuart Wheeler, Tank Museum, Bovington; Ian Proctor, Curator, Photographs, Imperial War Museum; Amanda Moreno, Curator, Royal Irish Fusiliers Museum, Armagh; Roy Walker and Terence Nelson, Royal Ulster Rifles Museum, Belfast; Allison Milligan and Gemma Ward, SE Education and Library Board, Ballynahinch; Brian Attwood, Editor, the *Stage*; Gordon Irving, Glasgow; Glyn Davies, Emkay Lothian Entertainments, Scotland; Paul Kane, Glasgow City Council Media Department; Dick Gilbert, Shane Conway and Ronnie Henry; Patrick Clarke, Newcastle (www.drumaroadhistory.com); David Corbett, Tyrella House, Tyrella; Bob Montgomery, Dublin; Brian Hoey, Newcastle Library; the Very Rev. Peter O'Hare, Annalong; Dick Gilbert, Shane Conway and Ronnie Henry (UK and Irish bus historians); Newcastle Chamber of Commerce website and BBC Northern Ireland (Your Place and Mine website). I would also like to pay very special tribute to my wife, Bernadette, for all her help and assistance while I was writing this book.

Further Reading

The newspaper and books listed below were used by the author during his research. None are available from Stenlake Publishing; please contact your local bookshop or reference library.

The Mourne Observer.
Belfast and Ulster Town Directory, 1910.
E. Estyn Evans, *Mourne Country - Landscape and Life in South Down*, 1967.
M.L. Kennedy and D.B. McNeill, *Early Bus Services in Ulster*, 1997.
David Kirk, *The Mountains of Mourne*, 2005.
Alexander Knox, *A History of County Down*, 1875.
Samuel Lewis, *Topographical Directory of Ireland*, 1837.
Harry McCaw and Brum Henderson, *Royal County Down Golf Club*, 1988.

Grenfell Morton, *Victorian & Edwardian Newcastle*, 1989.
Newcastle Urban District Council, *Your Guide to Newcastle*, c.1960.
Philip Orr, *The Road to the Somme*, 1987.
Earl of Roden, *Tollymore - the Story of an Irish Demesne*, 2005.

INTRODUCTION

Fronted by a beach that stretches for about eight kilometres and backed by the spectacular Mountains of Mourne, Newcastle, Co. Down, is one of Northern Ireland's leading seaside resorts with a setting unequalled by few others in all of Ireland. The development of the town dates back to the castle built by Felix Magennis in 1588, just south of the Shimna River and just to the west of what is now Newcastle's Main Street. This castle was demolished about 1830 to make way for the Annesley Arms Hotel, a building that subsequently became the public library. While Newcastle's early period was dominated by the Magennis clan, subsequent history owed much to two aristocratic families - the Annesleys and the Rodens.

William Annesley bought the Newcastle estate from Anthony Magennis in 1747 and the family became significant benefactors to the town. Lord Annesley built Donard Lodge about 1830 and in the years that followed he began to make moves to develop the town as a resort. Unfortunately, the house was largely destroyed by a fire towards the end of the Second World War and the ruins were finally demolished in September 1966.

The vast Tollymore demesne of the Earls of Roden was equally important in the history of the Newcastle area. The earliest mention of Tollymore dates from 1611 when the Magennis family received a grant of several townlands from King James I. The Hamiltons owned the land from about 1685 until 1798, when it was transferred to the first Earl of Roden, who had married into the Hamilton family.

In the early nineteenth century, Newcastle was still a small fishing village with a population of around 1,000. The opening up of granite quarries in the nearby mountains and the building of the harbour (a small part of the cost of which was paid by Lord Annesley) helped to expand the town, but as late as the mid 1840s Newcastle didn't consist of much more than a long straggling line of villas and humble thatched cottages for the fishing folk. But it did have seawater baths, with separate baths for the trades and the working class - the earliest sign of tourist development. The first major step came when the railway finally arrived in Newcastle in 1869, bringing the first day trippers from Belfast. Often, poor children from the city were brought to Newcastle for the day by such organisations as Grosvenor Hall, Belfast.

During the latter part of the nineteenth century and into the twentieth, the centre of Newcastle, with its Main Street and promenades, developed into a classic seaside resort, with many hotels and boarding houses and entertainments such as pierrot shows, dodgems, a boating lake, cafés, ice cream shops and amusement arcades. The local golf club was formed in 1889, now the world-class Royal County Down Golf Club, and in 1898 the Belfast & Co. Down Railway Company opened the Slieve Donard Hotel, designed to attract the luxury end of the tourist market. It is still there today, much improved and expanded under the ownership of the Hastings Hotel Group. One feature created in the 1880s, but long since vanished, was an ambitious switchback railway. Percy French, who wrote the world-famous song 'Where the Mountains of Mourne Sweep Down to the Sea', had many connections with Newcastle through his first wife, a member of the Annesley family, and he did much to help popularise the resort, often performing there as an entertainer. The town remained an immensely popular resort well into the 1960s with such places of amusement and entertainment as the Ritz cinema, the Central Ballroom, St Mary's Hall and the Annesley Hall.

In the early 1960s a young man was employed in a summer job at the Savoy Café in Newcastle; his name was Seamus Heaney, Nobel Prize-winner and one of the world's leading poets. In an earlier era, Richard Rowley (1877 - 1947), known as the 'Poet of the Mournes' spent much of his life in Newcastle. In the present day, Sean Rafferty from Newcastle is well known as a renowned classical music expert and a presenter on BBC Radio 3. Newcastle has always presented a combination of popular seaside culture and more intellectual pursuits, with an avid devotion to entertainment and performance; the Newcastle Amateur Dramatic Society was founded in 1947 and the locally based Glee Singers have been going strong since the 1950s. Since 1949 the town has had its own weekly newspaper, the *Mourne Observer*, which today is the largest selling weekly newspaper in south Co. Down.

The advent of the Troubles in Northern Ireland at the end of the 1960s brought 30 years of misery and strife across the area and innumerable tragedies to all parts of the community. Newcastle and district suffered along with the whole country but the town has always had a history of good community relations, as can be seen in the *Mourne Observer*, where local events, 'Orange' or 'Green', vie for space. Notices for local classes in Irish run alongside reports from local Orange lodges.

The Troubles also had a devastating effect on the tourism industry in Northern Ireland, but happily there are signs of a revival and regeneration well under way, not least in Newcastle where the most obvious is the new promenade that has been built in recent years. There is a new pedestrian bridge over the River Shimna and towards the end of 2006 an ambitious make-over plan was announced to improve the Main Street area of the town. Other modern tourist facilities include the Newcastle Centre and Tropicana on the seafront, as well as the seaweed baths in a Victorian terrace on the south promenade, the first such facility in Northern Ireland, while projects in the pipeline include the planned building of the Donard Drome, a huge indoor arena. The town now has a population of nearly 8,000 and there has also been rapid development of new apartments and houses. It is clear that soon Newcastle will once again regain its mantle as one of Ireland's premier seaside resorts.

On the right of this view of Main Street is the Presbyterian church, built around 1842. This photograph was taken after substantial remodelling was completed in 1909, work which included the addition of a larger and more ornate tower than the original. There are plans for further development, due to take place in 2008. The church formerly had cottages running alongside, but by about 1910 these had been replaced by the terraced villas seen here, most of which were run as guest houses.

Main Street, looking north, c.1920. At the far end of the street, on the left-hand side, can be seen the tower of the Presbyterian church, then the bulk of the Donard Buildings, complete with hotel. Just visible on the right-hand side is the steeple of St Mary's. The shop on the left was a chemist's; note the oversized mortar and pestle above the entrance. At this time, two of Main Street's better-known catering establishments were Murray's Café, which did lunches, dinners and teas, while Rodger's restaurant was regarded as more salubrious. The street today has a wide selection of shops and entertainment places for tourists, as well as the Newcastle Art Gallery. The Four Seasons shopping centre is on the site of the former manse for the Presbyterian Church (which cannot be seen in this view); the manse has since moved to Shimna Road.

The post office in this photograph was built towards the end of the nineteenth century by Priscilla McCoach who died in 1939; she was the grandmother of well-known local estate agent, Will Wilson. Before this post office was opened, she ran one at Causeway Road. The central promenade post office survived until 1959, when a new building was opened opposite the Municipal offices. That lasted until 2005 (many will remember sub-postmaster Willie McGivern who retired that year) and the current Donard Post Office can be found in Railway Street. On the left of the photograph is the Central Temperance Hotel; in the late nineteenth century, when it was owned by John Kerr, a clause in the freehold agreement banned the manufacture of candles on the premises! Subsequently, the hotel was owned by Annie McKee, who ran it with the help of Dorothy Hughes. It was long popular with visitors to Newcastle; perhaps a reason for this could be seen in a 1935 advertisement which mentioned 'hot and cold water baths - free'! The hotel was demolished in the 1970s and Arcadia Amusements was built on the site.

This photograph of the promenade was taken in the early 1930s. The bus belonged to the Mourne Bus Company, which was owned by Tommy and Davy McAtee who ran a garage together at Greencastle Street in Kilkeel. It was a small company, with just five buses in its fleet, and one of its main routes was from Kilkeel to Belfast via Newcastle, beginning in 1926. (Before going into buses, Davy McAtee had run a hairdressing business in Kilkeel.) The roads in those days were poorly surfaced and the buses had little suspension and solid studded tyres, so a journey was often an uncomfortable experience; in winter rugs were supplied to regular passengers going to and from Belfast. In 1933 the McAtees were bought out by the Belfast Omnibus Company and when the Northern Ireland Road Transport Board came into being in October 1935, nationalising the many small privately owned bus companies in the province, the pioneering days of bus travel came to an end. At the turn of the twentieth century local people were reliant on horse-drawn cars, to destinations like Rostrevor and Warrenpoint, while a jarvey car brought people from Castlewellan to the station in Newcastle. After the First World War, however, close to 30 private bus companies operated in Co. Down alone.

The bandstand seen in this photograph from March 1962 was built in the early twentieth century and remained a popular gathering place for summer crowds for most of that century. It was subsequently removed and can now be seen on the National Trust-owned estate at Rowallane, Co. Down. John Elmore ran the successful Pierrot shows that were staged on the bandstand in the years after World War II until about 1960. He died in 1987.

The promenade on a summer's day in the mid-twentieth century. In the far distance is the towering bulk of the Slieve Donard Hotel.

Bathing huts on the beach in a view taken close to Black Rock, with the Mountains of Mourne rising up in the background.

Another view of the beach, probably in the late 1950s or early 1960s, with the bandstand to the right and St John's Church of Ireland at Black Rock in the distance.

A grateful town had this memorial fountain, which no longer exists, built to honour the memory and work of Percy French (1854 - 1920) whose famous song written in 1896 about the Mountains of Mourne sweeping down to the sea helped put Newcastle on the tourism map. French, born in Co. Roscommon, began as a civil engineer and inspector of drains before starting a long and successful career as a songwriter and entertainer. He was also a very able watercolour artist. He had close connections with Newcastle, as his first wife, Ettie (who subsequently died in childbirth) was the sister of Felicity, Countess of Annesley, and he was a frequent performer at the Slieve Donard Hotel. A new memorial to him was unveiled on the new promenade in 2007. French is buried far from his native land, at Formby in Lancashire, where in 1920 he died from pneumonia at the age of 65. Probably the best interpreter of his songs was the tenor Brendan O'Dowda, who was born in Dundalk in 1925 and died in Southampton in 2002.

The Royal County Down Golf Club began as a nine-hole course in 1889, after a meeting in the hall of Mr Lawrence's dining rooms in Newcastle, presided over by Lord Annesley. It quickly expanded to eighteen holes that same year and the first professional was appointed in 1890. A weekly 'golfers' express' service was established to bring golfers by rail from Belfast to the club and a nine-hole ladies course was created by 1907. In 1908 the club was allowed to use the prefix 'Royal' in its name, courtesy of King Edward VII. Today, the club has two eighteen-hole courses; the Championship course is widely regarded as being among the top ten golf courses in the world, while the Annesley is considered less challenging. In 1895 it was decided to build a new clubhouse to replace the accommodation provided for golfers at the nearby railway station. The new clubhouse, designed in the Old English style, was opened on 11 September 1897 with a gala banquet attended by over 300 members and their guests. Included on the menu were hare soup and grouse. At the time, the new clubhouse was described as being 'by far and away the best clubhouse in Ireland'. In December 1914, Francis, sixth Earl Annesley and second president of the club, was killed when the plane he was flying in to France crashed into the English Channel. This photograph was probably taken in the 1930s and shows the clubhouse from a southerly aspect; the entrance to the members' changing rooms is beneath the steps leading to the main entrance. A major extension to the clubhouse was built in 1960. Another elegant game flourished in Newcastle in the early twentieth century when the town had its own croquet club.

The ninth green on the original eighteen-hole course at Royal County Down. The course layout has changed considerably over the years and at one time the ninth hole was the seventeenth. Today it is the putting green.

This aerial photograph of Newcastle, taken in the early 1930s, gives an idea of how the general area, particularly the lower half of what is shown here, has developed over the years. In the centre can be seen the Donard Hotel, still in business today; it dates back to around 1880 and in its earlier days was known as the Donard Buildings' Hotel. In 1910 the owner of the hotel was listed as Patrick McCartan, while the manager was a man called Brady. The hotel has been owned by the Maginn family since 1946; other hoteliers in the town include the Irwin family who run the Avoca Hotel on the central promenade. On the right-hand side of Main Street can be seen the square tower of the Presbyterian church, while further along Main Street, on the left-hand side, is St Mary's Church.

Shimna Road in Newcastle was officially opened on 16 May 1930 by Lady Mabel Annesley. It was built because Main Street, even then, was becoming congested with motorised traffic and a bypass road was needed to run parallel with it. Two local firms, Keowns of Moyado and Isaac Hamilton of Annalong, built the road at a cost of £10,000 (a contingency sum of £500 was put into the contract, in case costs ran over, but it was never used). A new type of tarmacadam was used and two bridges were built over the River Shimna. The stones for the roadway came from the Small family's farm near Castlewellan, while the granite kerbs came from the nearby Hamilton quarry. At the time, many complaints were heard that the footpaths on the new road had been made too narrow. Built at a time of widespread unemployment in Northern Ireland, the Shimna Road project was designated a 'green card scheme' for local unemployed men while skilled tradespeople were employed by the two contractors. The houses were built at the same time and construction of those continued after completion of the road.

The war memorial in Newcastle, built to commemorate those from the locality who had fallen in the First World War, was designed as a sphinx on a plain pedestal and was created by Francis Wiles, a noted sculptor of the time. It is the only war memorial in Northern Ireland featuring a lion. It was sited in front of the Newcastle bathhouse, which later became the offices of Newcastle Urban District Council. Up to 1928, when the memorial was unveiled, Armistice Day was marked at Black Rock beside a captured German gun. In 1947 the war memorial was moved and unveiled at its present location outside the Annesley Buildings and the tourist information office. While this area is in the process of being improved, it is expected that the small remembrance garden will be retained. The memorial itself has 25 names from the First World War and seventeen from the Second World War.

Railway Street, Newcastle, Co. Down.

Railway Street, close to the former railway station and running down to the seafront, still has a variety of shops on it, including a newsagent, a music and book shop, a travel shop, a wool shop, a taxi firm and a furniture shop for St Vincent de Paul, a leading charitable organisation.

Co. Down, Railway Station, Newcastle. M. 256.

By 1850 the Belfast & County Down Railway extended as far as Newtownards and Comber. However, progress south of Comber was slow because of the difficult terrain and the railway didn't reach Downpatrick until 1861. The line to Newcastle was finally opened on 26 March 1869 and the railway station was completed that year. The station lasted until 1906, when it was replaced by a new building shown here. The railway line from Belfast to Newcastle closed in 1950, after which the building was turned into a bus station. Today, the striking clock tower has been preserved in working order while the station building houses a Lidl supermarket. In 1906 the Great Northern Railway arrived in the town with its line from Banbridge, sharing the same station and its replacement.

Building work on the Slieve Donard Hotel started in 1896 and it was opened on 24 June 1898, having cost around £84,000 paid for by the Belfast & County Down Railway Company. The Gothic-style building still dominates the northern skyline of Newcastle, and when it opened it was a remarkably self-contained operation with such facilities as a vegetable garden, piggery, Turkish baths and laundry, as well as coal fires in all bedrooms. Over the years, the hotel has attracted many famous personalities, from Charlie Chaplin to Alan Wicker, Daniel O'Donnell to Tiger Woods. In 1972 the Slieve Donard was one of six railway hotels in Northern Ireland that were bought for £1 million by the Hastings Hotel Group. Today, it is the only one of the six that's still functioning as a hotel. In its early days as part of the group, the hotel incurred such losses that Dr Billy Hastings, the founder and now chairman of Hastings Hotels, referred to it as the 'Titanic'. However, in recent years much investment in new facilities such as a spa and many more bedrooms have turned the hotel into Northern Ireland's equivalent of the Gleneagles Hotel in Scotland. Subsequently, many smaller hotels opened in the town, such as the Burrendale in 1978.

In 1837 Samuel Lewis, in his *Topographical Dictionary of Ireland*, reported that the harbour in Newcastle was used mainly for the export of oats, barley and potatoes, with large quantities being shipped to Dublin and Liverpool. At that stage, the harbour was a relatively new concern, having been built only a decade earlier at a cost of £30,000. Lord Annesley had contributed £2,000. As Lewis stated, '. . . the harbour is accessible at high water to vessels of large burden and has been very beneficial to the trade of the town.' The harbour also had an export trade in granite from a quarry in the Mournes that had been opened in 1824; the granite was taken by horse-drawn railcars down to the pier for export. And yet, by the end of the 1890s the harbour was in a ruinous state, mainly due to severe storms over the years. It is now used by a small number of fishing boats and pleasure craft - the Newcastle sailing club is close by - while every year it is dredged to keep it clear. Newcastle's sewage treatment plant is located close to the harbour and it has helped keep the town beach clean; however, the beach has been badly eroded over the past half century. The Harbour Residents Association says that the treatment plant needs expansion, and claims that the harbour is the only one in Northern Ireland not to have had any money spent on it in recent years. After a ferocious storm in 2002, when part of a seawall collapsed, elaborate plans began to be made for the new promenade, which now stretches from the Slieve Donard Hotel to close by the Glen River.

Old schooners at the harbour. Close by is Widow's Row (not shown in this photograph), built for the families left fatherless by the great storm of January 1843. A total of 73 men were lost - fishermen from Newcastle and lower Mourne, as well as would-be rescuers - when sixteen fishing boats were overwhelmed by the storm. The houses are still there today, some rented out as tourist accommodation.

Black Rock, the area on the southern side of Newcastle, derives its name from the black shingle on the beach close by. The nearby St John's Church of Ireland, whose spire can just be seen on the right, dates from 1832, having been built at a cost of £1,200 (originally estimated at £700) and paid for by William Richard, Earl Annesley. Black Rock has long been noted for what is believed to be the oldest outdoor swimming pool in Ireland. In 1910 the Newcastle Urban District Council, then not long in existence, cleared away the trees and the shrubs from the enclosed public area at Black Rock.

This chasm on the coastline close to Newcastle has a colourful legend attached to it. It is named after a young woman called Maggie, who is said to have jumped from one side of the chasm to the other while being chased by either a suitor, bull or witch, depending on which folk story you care to believe. She did the jump while she was carrying a basket of eggs and when she landed on the far side, not one of them was broken. Just beyond Maggie's Leap is Armour's Hole, a cleft in the rock where in 1701 a young man is supposed to have murdered his father in a row over a young woman.

A horse-drawn bread van turning into the Tollymore estate near Newcastle, some time between 1900 and 1910. The bakery's name has been blacked out, but the Hovis brand name is clearly visible. At this stage, Hovis bread had already been popular in Northern Ireland for over 20 years. However, the van could well have come from the Belfast-based Ormo bakery, which had a depot in Newcastle for many years. In the early twentieth century the Belfast area had about 25 large bakeries, while the rest of what is now Northern Ireland had 35. Today, Belfast has just two plant bakeries, while the Portadown area has one. However, the Strand bakery and restaurant, set up on the central promenade in Newcastle by the Nugent family in 1930, is still going strong.

The Youth's Hostel at Bloody Bridge, in the "Kingdom of Mourne."

The first youth hostel in the Mountains of Mourne was formally opened on 5 May 1934 by the then Stormont Minister of Education, Lord Charlemont. The wooden structure was built by the members themselves and the first warden was Felix O'Neill, on whose farm the hostel was built. The hostel had a common room and a self-catering kitchen, and dormitories for fourteen men and fourteen women on each side of the common room. The hostel closed in 1966.

This is the Slievenaman youth hostel, also wooden built and close to Bryansford. Other hostels in the Mournes included Knockbarragh at Rostrevor and those at Minerstown and Kinahalla. The latter was opened in 1959. Today, Hostelling International Northern Ireland has just one hostel in the area, in Newcastle at No. 30 Downs Road, not far from Railway Street.

Glenada on the south promenade has been used by the YMCA as a centre for Christian witness, teaching and fellowship since 1900. The ground on which the house stands was leased by the Dean of Dromore from the Earl of Annesley's estate in 1879 and the house came to be known as the Bishop's House. In 1900 the then owners of the house, Mr and Mrs Harold Gray, finding that it was too big for their own use, decided to lease it to the YMCA for one shilling a year. Glenada opened as a Christian holiday home on 28 July 1900 and in the early years of the twentieth century it was a popular destination for mill girls from Belfast who couldn't afford a holiday by the sea in more luxurious accommodation. One of the key figures in Glenada for many years was Margaret Livingstone, who arrived to live and work in 1923 and spent the rest of her life there. She died in 1971, aged 98. In recent years, the YMCA and the YMCA of Ireland have continued to work together to further develop Glenada and its facilities.

Military bands were a popular sight and sound in the Newcastle area in the early twentieth century; they were attached to regiments stationed at nearby Ballykinlar. Usually they were elaborate ensembles, including drums, fifes and pipes, as in this photograph of a Royal Irish Fusiliers' band, seen in a field just outside Bryansford.

Tyrella Restaurant, near Tyrella Strand, was a popular stopping off point in the 1950s, especially for touring buses. The corrugated-iron roofed building was established by a local man called Patterson, who had worked at the nearby army camp, and a man called Ritchie then took over the running of the restaurant, noted for its teas and ice cream. It later closed and the building was taken over by the Downshire Hospital in Downpatrick, converting it into a hostel for use by some of its patients. It has been vacant since the 1980s.

This garage was close to the Tyrella Restaurant which was run by a man called Patterson who also had a bicycle sales and repair shop. He subsequently sold this shop to a local businessman called Joe Trainor, who developed the premises into the garage. Not only did it service cars and sell petrol and oil, but it even sold newspapers and tickets for the shore cars that ran at Tyrella and Rathmullan. Beside the petrol pump on the left the structure with the sloping roof was an oil-dispensing stand. In the 1930s, oil for cars was sold loose from this type of stand, poured into a measure. The oil was often supplied by a company called Wakefields, better known today as Castrol.

Tyrella beach, about 10 kilometres north-east of Newcastle as the crow flies (a much longer distance by road), remains one of the most popular beaches on the Co. Down coastline. The wide and flat sandy beach (which today has a Blue Flag) stretches for several kilometres and is backed by about 25 hectares of sand dunes. In those sand dunes can still be seen traces of the trenches that were dug during military training over the years of the First World War. Long ago, Tyrella also had a coastguard station, but this was closed down in 1909. Also well known in this area is the Ballykinlar Gaelic Athletic Association club, founded in 1932; its Memorial Park was opened in 1956. Before the club opened, cricket was the most popular sport in the area.

On 7 September 1914, just over a month after the start of the First World War, recruiting began for the 36th (Ulster) Division of Lord Kitchener's army of volunteers, who were to be trained and sent to the front to fight the German armies. The men in the 36th (Ulster) Division were drawn primarily from the Ulster Volunteer Force, set up by Lord Carson to fight against Irish home rule. Four battalions - the 8th, 9th, 10th and 11th Royal Irish Rifles - were sent to the army camp at Ballykinlar to begin training and several thousand mainly working class men from Belfast were accommodated in these tents. Sometimes, the men had excursions into Newcastle, where misbehaviour and fighting in the streets happened on occasions. Little did these men know what fate was in store for them. During the Battle of the Somme, which lasted from July to November 1916, over one million soldiers from both sides were killed; on the very first day, 1 July, the 36th (Ulster) Division had 5,500 casualties, of whom about 2,000 were killed. The Division was made up of nine battalions of the Royal Irish Rifles, three of the Royal Inniskilling Fusiliers and one of the Royal Irish Fusiliers.

This field kitchen was set up at Ballykinlar camp to feed the thousands of recruits stationed there for training. The large vat-like containers with chimneys were used for cooking food, which was then distributed in the smaller containers seen in the foreground.

Potatoes, often served with Irish stew, were a staple of the monotonous military diet for the trainee volunteers at Ballykinlar; vast quantities were consumed, so peeling them was a task that occupied many of the soldiers when they weren't training for the battles to come.

This car and the three curious tank-like vehicles are pictured on the beach close to Ballykinlar in the mid to late 1930s. The military vehicles are in fact examples of the Vickers-Carden-Loyd utility tractor used by the infantry battalions then stationed at the nearby army camp.

The Sandes Homes were set up close to military barracks to offer young soldiers places for entertainment and self-improvement, in a Christian atmosphere, as an alternative to public houses. Elise Sandes, who founded the homes, was born in Tralee, Co. Kerry, in 1851 and the first Sandes Home was opened in Cork in 1877. After the establishment of the Irish Free State in 1922, most of the homes in that part of Ireland closed down. Elise Sandes then moved to the Sandes Home beside the army camp at Ballykinlar. She died there in 1933 and was buried at nearby Tyrella with full military honours. Her tombstone is inscribed: 'For 66 years the friend of soldiers'. At the Sandes Home in Ballykinlar, Elise Sandes was succeeded by another equally remarkable woman, Eva Maguire, pictured here, who died at Ballykinlar on 27 October 1967 and was accorded the same honours as her predecessor. The original Sandes Home at Ballykinlar was built in 1901; in 1974 it was burned down during an IRA attack, although it was subsequently rebuilt.

Harry Ferguson was the pioneer of flying in Ireland. Born in 1884, he made his first powered flight at Hillsborough, Co. Down, in 1909, when he flew for 118.5 metres. Then, in 1910, the town of Newcastle offered £100 for the first flight along the beach in front of the Slieve Donard Hotel. Ferguson eagerly accepted the challenge; the first take-off ended in failure, but eventually he did make the flight for about five kilometres at heights that varied from 15 to 90 metres, winning the prize. A granite memorial to his pioneering flight stands on the north promenade in Newcastle. Subsequently, Ferguson became world famous for his development work with agricultural tractors.

Newcastle has had a lifeboat since 1830, but the first only lasted until 1833 when it was removed. Some 20 years later, the Earl of Annesley paid for a replacement and Newcastle has had a lifeboat ever since. The self-righting lifeboat seen in this photograph from March 1906 was the *Farnley*, which had been in service since 1881. Later that year it was replaced by the *Marianne*, another self-righting boat. A modern lifeboat house was built at the harbour in 1936 and was used as such until 1993, when a new house and slipway were opened.

HERBERT HALPIN'S ENTERTAINERS
NEWCASTLE · SEASON · 1909

Herbert Halpin, a local man from Kilcoo, six kilometres south-west of Castlewellan, had a popular semi-professional troupe of artistes who were a popular attraction on the seafront in Newcastle in the years before the First World War. Even though the performances were popular and the troupe often featured on postcards of the time, little history has been preserved about Halpin and his co-performers. In this photograph they are seen on a makeshift stage at the seafront during the summer of 1909 (the bandstand would not be open for another year). Halpin had many years' experience as a professional entertainer, having been long and closely connected with the Empire Theatre in Victoria Square, Belfast, one of the city's principal theatres for music hall and variety around the start of the twentieth century. The last version of the theatre building had opened in 1894 and it closed down in 1961. In later decades, Newcastle became renowned for its Pierrot shows at the bandstand.

This must have been one of the earliest family outings by motor car in the Newcastle area. The 1902 French-made Panhard et Levassor car was probably bought in Belfast and judging from its excellent condition must have been almost new when this photograph was taken. This marque was one of the most popular before the First World War; the last civilian Panhard car was made in 1967, although the name lives on today in military vehicles.

Ballymartin is a small seaside village about 20 kilometres south of Newcastle. In the *Belfast & Ulster Towns Directory* of 1910, just twelve residents were listed. A sub post office was opened there in 1904 and subsequently run by the Newell family for 68 years. In the old days, Ballymartin Bridge was a noted meeting place for local people on fine evenings, when accordions were often played. The local church, St Joseph's, dates back to 1902; it replaced the first Catholic church in the village, built in 1785 in what is now the middle of the present graveyard (it had been reconstructed in 1825).

This peaceful photograph of Dolly's Brae, about eleven kilometres from Newcastle, belies the battle that took place close to here in July 1849. After 12 July celebrations that year, opposing factions started fighting and soldiers were sent to protect the small village. However, five Catholics were killed and many local homes as well as the Catholic church were set on fire. However, the Orange Order survived the disgrace of Dolly's Brae and revived itself in the 1860s.

The Bryansford Gate at the entrance to the Tollymore estate, and close to Bryansford, was built in the Gothic style in 1786. The wrought-iron gates were added a century later. The small porter's office beside the gate had a visitors' book that everyone had to sign; by 1900 the demesne inside was open to the public on Tuesdays and Fridays. Unusually, between the world wars, one of the gatekeepers was a woman, a Mrs McClelland. The original gate lodge was built in 1802, extended in 1859 and again in the 1970s. The structure in the background, behind the gates, is a small folly.

The charming village of Bryansford, three kilometres south of Castlewellan. The cottages seen here in the Main Street are among the group originally built for workers on the nearby Tollymore estate of the Earl of Roden; they lived there rent free. The village's first Catholic church, St Patrick's, was built in 1760, complete with thatched roof. It was replaced by the 1831 church, to which the Earl of Roden contributed. A girls' school opened in the village in 1822, supported by the Countess of Roden, while the boys' school began in 1826. In the nineteenth century, facilities in Bryansford included a baker, a grocer and a Bible repository, as well as a hotel. Today, the village still has McConnell's shop and post office, but the study centre next door (see next page) to it is now closed and due to be redeveloped.

This striking house at Bryansford was built about 1830 for the Dowager Countess Roden, sister of the Earl of Clanbrassil. Subsequently, it was used for many years as the rectory attached to the Church of Ireland church in Kilcoo. During the 1920s a Miss Davidson lived in the house; she was very interested in drama and was a leading light in the Newcastle Amateur Dramatic Society. She eventually went to live in Co. Wicklow. The house was converted into a field study centre in 1973 and remained in use as such until 2002. It was then boarded up and, at the time of writing in 2007, the future use of the site remains undecided.

Slieve Bingian or Binnian (*Sliábh Binneain* in Irish) stands 747 metres above sea level and is the third highest mountain in Northern Ireland. With the rocky tors on its peak, from which it derives its name, it is one of the most distinctive mountains in the Mournes. Colligan Bridge, in the foreground of the photograph, crosses the Kilkeel River. The Binnian tunnel beneath the mountain is a unique engineering feat, built between 1947 and 1951 and designed to carry water from the Annalong valley to the Silent Valley reservoir. The two tunnelling teams started from opposite sides of the mountain and when they met in the middle, they were just five centimetres off course. The tunnel was officially opened on 28 August 28 1952. The Mountains of Mourne are partially owned by the National Trust and there has been much recent local controversy over plans to make the mountains the first national park in Northern Ireland.

In 1901 water from the Mournes was piped through to Belfast for the first time. Then, in 1904, work began on building the 35 kilometres long Mourne Wall, which delineated the Mourne Catchment area for the reservoirs. Work on the wall took eighteen years to complete; meanwhile, in 1910, it was decided that, with increasing demand for water in Belfast, the Silent Valley Reservoir would be built. Work started in 1923 and the reservoir, with 97 hectares of water, was officially opened in 1933.

Tullybrannigan is one of 22 townlands in Tollymore Ward. When this photograph was taken close to a century ago the area was very rural, but since the 1960s it has been much developed. The bridge in the photograph spans the small stream called Tullybrannigan River which flows into the Shimna River. At the time of this photograph the bridge was known as Laird's Bridge after a local farmer, but the moniker has long since passed out of use. In recent years, the road and bridge have been completely altered due to road realignment work.

Beside the main road from Newcastle to Annalong, the Ballagh tea rooms, run by the two Carey sisters, were a popular stopping off place for cyclists and tourists generally. The premises, which have long since been demolished, also had one of the earliest petrol pumps in the area.